Contents:

Martin Luther King

The Pastor Who Had a Daring Dream

1929 — 1968

*Great men and women are not in need of our praise.
We are the ones in need of getting to know them.*

By Sharon Jones
Illustrations by Andrea Jula

HEROES OF FAITH AND COURAGE CLASSICS
Scandinavia

IT WASN'T SUPPOSED
TO END THIS WAY

On the evening of April 3, 1968, it was difficult to push through the crowd that had gathered in Memphis to hear Martin Luther King, Jr. Once on the podium, King looked out over all eager faces. Then he bowed his head and thanked God for being chosen to lead the march later that week. He added a few words about their objectives. Then the tone of his speech changed unexpectedly.

"Some began to talk about the threats that were out, of what would happen to me," he intoned, "but it really doesn't matter to me now, because I've been to the mountain

top and I've seen the Promised Land. I may not get there with you, but I want you to know, tonight that we as a people will get to the Promised Land! So I'm happy tonight. I'm not worried about anything! I'm not fearing any man! Mine eyes have seen the glory of the coming of the Lord!"

The audience leapt to its feet, shouting, clapping, and cheering. But Dr. King's friends knew something was strangely different. He never concentrated so much of a speech on himself. They thought, "What's wrong with him? He is working much too hard. After the march, Dr. King needs a long rest."

That night Dr. King and his friend, Rev. Abernathy, were driven to the

Lorraine Motel on Mulberry Street. Dr. King would occupy room 306 on the second floor. His room had a balcony from which he could see the parking lot and pool, and from which he could communicate with his staff who occupied the rooms around his. Their presence served as a convenience as well as added security against violence. The plainclothes officers whose job it was to protect him, relaxed.

The next day, following meetings and strategy sessions, King and Abernathy had lunch in the motel, rested, and then began to dress for dinner. King stepped out onto the balcony to give last-minute instructions to his staff about the upcoming meeting. Rev. Abernathy stood in the balcony doorway to the rear. Then it happened.

A single gun shot was heard. Friends stared in disbelief as both Dr. King and Rev. Abernathy hit the floor. Time froze. Abernathy saw the figure sprawled beside him and hoped Dr. King had simply fallen to the floor in order to avoid the danger. But the position of King's body told a different, much more horrifying story.

Abernathy noticed that a bullet had hit King in the neck with such velocity that it knocked him flat on his back. On the balcony floor lay the man on whom all their hopes for continued victories over racial injustice had been pinned. The unbelievable fact slowly began to sink in. Dr. Martin Luther King, Jr. had just been assassinated.

4

WHAT'S IN A NAME?

A violent end was the farthest thing from the minds of Alberta Christine and Mike King, Sr. on January 15, 1929 when Mike Jr. was born to them. Their 15-month-old daughter had recently survived a severe illness and the young family was still growing. Only eighteen months later, Alfred Daniel (A.D.) was born. Still, Mike Sr. was working hard as assistant pastor at the prominent Ebenezer Baptist Church, doing his best to carve out a comfortable existence for his family. Family was important.

Since birth certificates were not commonly issued to black sharecropper families, Mike Sr. had never had one. His father insisted that he was originally named Martin Luther, after two of his father's brothers. "Names are important," Grandpa King would say. "They carry on the legacy of family. Names are especially important in

black families. We live in a society which allows us to have little else than family to be proud of." So, as Mike Sr. stood by his father's deathbed with 4-year-old Mike Jr., he had promised to take out the necessary legal papers. Soon after his father's death, Mike Sr. officially became Martin Luther King, Sr. and his son became Martin Luther King, Jr.

When the Depression of the thirties hit, the family had an important opportunity to put into action what was being preached. One night the children overheard their father telling a group from the church, "Do unto others as you would have them do unto you. This Depression has hit everybody hard. There are very few jobs for white people, so you know the Negro is having even worse luck. Let's use the church as a storehouse. Everyone can bring what they have–potatoes, tomatoes, carrots, blankets, diapers, anything. Then,

whoever needs something can simply exchange what they have for what they need."

The children got excited. Not remembering that they were supposed to be asleep in bed, they ran down the stairs and into the middle of the meeting, blurting out ideas they had for toys and clothes they could give away, The room grew silent. Rev. King approached the children and said sternly, "Aren't you supposed to be in bed? It's obvious that you have been eavesdropping."

The children froze. Then Martin Jr. spoke up. "We couldn't help overhearing. You always taught us to do whatever we could to help. That's the Bible way."

Daddy King's stern expression suddenly changed to one of pride as he pulled Martin close to him. "Did you hear the eagerness of these three children?" He looked straight into Martin's eyes. "Son," he said, "God has given you your heart to help others. There will come a day when you'll have your chance to make a real difference." Somehow, Martin knew his father was right.

SOMETHING CHANGES

As a child, Martin learned things quickly and, thanks to his mother's early teaching at home, was advanced when he entered first grade. Martin was already thinking of books as untiring teachers with amazing amounts of knowledge in them. When he secured a job as a paper boy delivering the Atlanta Journal, Martin started buying his own books.

There was so much to know, but there were some things Martin found hard to understand. One day, when

The King Children

The three King children had very different personalities. Christine, the oldest, seemed determined to follow in the footsteps of her mother and grandmother and pursue a teaching career. She was always eager to learn. The boys, Martin and A.D., were being groomed by their father and grandfather to keep up the family tradition and become ministers. A.D., the youngest, was boisterous and stubborn, but his father could see these traits being shaped into the qualities needed to be a fiery Baptist preacher. M.L., as Martin was called as a child, was a deep thinker with an inquisitive mind. Early in life he displayed great speaking skills and he also had a fine singing voice. His family knew that he would be a natural for the pulpit of Ebenezer Baptist Church.

Left: *Martin's birthplace in Atlanta, Georgia.* Right: *The King family 1939. Back row: Martin's mother, father and grandmother. Front row: A.D., Christine and M.L.K.*

he went over to a friend's house to play, the friend's mother stopped Martin at the door of her home. "Martin," she said, "I'm afraid you can't come into the house and play with Arthur anymore. Good-bye."

Martin just stood there as the screen door slammed shut. What had he done? As hot tears filled his eyes, he rushed on home.

His mother was busy squeezing lemons to make her famous home-made lemonade when Martin appeared at the screen door. She noticed right away that something was terribly wrong. Taking both of his shoulders in her hands and kneeling down beside him, she asked, "Martin, what happened? What has upset you so?"

For a moment or two, Martin could only stare at her as the tears burned his eyes and streamed over his cheeks. Finally he shouted, "Why Momma, why? Arthur is my best friend. Every day we ride our bikes or play ball. I've always been good around his house. What did I do? Why did they say I can't go there anymore? Why Momma, why?"

Martin's mother hugged and rocked him for a long time. She knew very well what was wrong. But how could she tell her sensitive, innocent seven-year-old child that he had reached the age when some thought the races should be separated? Once you reached a certain age, white people simply did not associate with black people as friends and equals.

"Martin," his mother began, "many things in this world are done that shouldn't be done. Separating people from their friends because of the color of their skin is one of them."

The puzzled look would not leave Martin's face. Alberta King looked him straight in the eye. Her tone was gentle yet determined. "Now you listen to me," she said. "People who try to make you feel like you are less of a person just don't know the truth. The truth is, everyone is the same, equal, in God's eyes. And God's opinion is the only opinion that matters. You did nothing wrong. It is this system of separation that is wrong. You're as good as anyone else."

With that, his mother went back to squeezing the lemonade, but now she was humming "We Shall Overcome."

"YOU'RE AS GOOD AS ANYONE ELSE"

Since the abolition of slavery, the Southern states had come up with a system in which blacks and whites lived under different rules. Martin was familiar with separate entrances to stores, separate seating in movie theaters, separate elevators and staircases in public buildings, and water fountains marked "Whites Only" or "Colored Only."

Martin's parents were determined to raise their children with a sense of dignity no matter how they were treated by others. Blacks were expected to bow their heads and slouch their shoulders in public, but Martin saw his father always walking tall and proud through the streets of Atlanta. One time when he went shopping with his father, Martin saw a pair of shoes that he wanted in the store window. He and his father entered the store through the front entrance.

A clerk ran up to them shouting, "If

you want something, come in through the back of the store like the other niggers do." "Nigger" was a very degrading word white people used to insult black people.

Martin's father had stood firm and looked the man straight in the eye. "If you cannot sell us these shoes here in the front of the store " he said, "we will take our money elsewhere." Then Martin felt his dad's strong hand on his shoulder as they left the store, by the front door.

Martin looked up and saw the sad look in his father's eyes. "Some people think they are better than others simply because of the color of their skin. They have thought this for a long time and have convinced themselves that this is true." The sad look turned to one of proud determination. "Son, don't you ever believe that any one person is better than any other person. Especially son, remember that you are just as good as anyone else."

They were both silent as they got into the car to go home, but their thoughts were disturbed when a police officer stopped them. When the officer walked up to the car, he motioned for Martin's father to roll down his window. "Listen, boy," the officer began. Before he could finish his statement, Martin's father interrupted him. Pointing at Martin, he faced the officer and said, "That is a boy, I am a man."

Martin never forgot that lesson. He decided then and there that he would work with his father to put an end to the terrible system of racial separation.

Above: *Martin's father preaching at Ebenezer Baptist Church.* Right: *Crozer Theological Seminary in Pennsylvania where Martin studied to become a pastor.*

IT'S DIFFERENT UP NORTH

Martin entered college when he was just fifteen years old. During his sophomore year, his parents allowed him and his brother A.D. to work one summer in the tobacco fields up north in Connecticut. The plentiful work, good pay, and curiosity about the North drove many Southern young people to the area. Although the work was hard, the bosses tended to be fair. The most amazing thing to Martin was experiencing whites, blacks and immigrants sweating side by side as equals. They strung young plants together, picked the large tobacco leaves together, and carried the full lathes to the shed rafters together.

One weekend, he and A.D. decided to relax by going to the movies. After they paid for their tickets, the usher

Martin's Schooling

Martin's mother, Alberta King, taught her children at home until they entered first grade. Between the ages of 5 and 11, Martin attended public school and was at the top of his class every year. When he was eleven, he was enrolled in a school for exceptionally bright children. He loved this school and advanced at an even faster rate. Unfortunately, the school closed two years later. In those days, black children and white children were not allowed to attend school together, so Martin had to transfer to the all-black high school near his home. By this time, he was three years ahead of his classmates. After just a couple of years of high school, Martin was accepted as a freshman at Morehouse College. He was only fifteen years old.

Martin graduated from Morehouse College when he was nineteen. There was still much more that he wanted to learn. He attended two more schools and graduated with his master's degree from Crozer Theological Seminary and obtained his doctorate from Boston College.

directed them to their seats. "A.D., does something seem strange to you?" Martin asked as they eased into their seats.

"Yeah Martin," A.D. replied. "I think that usher sat us in the wrong section. These seats don't feel like 'Colored Section' seats. Look! These seats are clean with full cushions and no exposed springs " They both laughed.

At the end of that summer, Martin and A.D. left to go back to Atlanta as two changed young men. On the train headed home they reminisced about the back-breaking work they had endured, the friends they had made and money they had earned Mostly, though, they talked about the phenomenon of racial equality. Then something happened.

As they approached the Atlanta city limits, the conductor came up to Martin, A.D., and the other black

passengers. "You boys are going to have to move to the back of the dining car now."

The other black people did as they were told, but Martin sat paralyzed in his seat. He was surprised at his anger. It was as if now that equality was being snatched away from him, it felt even better than he had realized.

The conductor stood over Martin and began to shout, "What's the matter, boy? I don't want any trouble out of you. Now move to the back!"

Martin's feet felt like lead as he dragged himself to the back of the car. He and his friends said nothing as the conductor pulled a screen to separate them from the white passengers. Martin thought, "Only ten minutes ago we were passengers just like everybody else. How can our presence be so offensive now, that others can't even see us?"

CHOOSING THE MINISTRY AS A CAREER

Morehouse College was a place to study in preparation for the ministry. Martin wanted a college education, but he didn't want to spend his life behind a pulpit. His father was now senior pastor of Ebenezer and both he and A.D. were feeling the pressure to follow in their father's footsteps. Martin loved the Church, but he disagreed with the strict standards of behavior he was expected to uphold and he realized these standards would become even stricter if he entered the ministry. During his early college years, he found himself often bragging about how he intended to be free of these rules as an adult.

"Going to another dance tonight, Martin?" asked Philip, his roommate. Philip laughed as he casually leaned against the door frame, chomping on an apple. "You're going to dance holes in your shoes."

"Yeah, I can hear my father now. 'Good Baptists don't dance to the devil music. It destroys your brain and corrupts your soul '" Martin smiled as he straightened his tie. "But seriously, all that hand-waving, foot-stomping, and yelling 'Amen' isn't going to free the Negro from segregation. In the Bible, God helped people in their real-life situations. If He's the same God, He'll do the same for us just because He loves us, not because we obey a bunch of man-made rules."

Martin loved his social life, but he loved God more. He prayed often about what God wanted him to do with his life. By the spring of his senior year at Morehouse, Martin reached a decision. Through his classes and from listening to mentors like Dr. Benjamin Mays, Martin knew that God wanted him to reach blacks with the Bible's message as it related

to their present problems. He also realized that the Church was the strongest institution that the white power structure did not control. At church, blacks were free to talk, cry, rejoice, and complain about anything.

So, even though the Church was strongly traditional, Martin knew he would become a minister. Changes in accepted traditions came about slowly. So since no one would listen to his words if his actions upset them, he decided to renounce dating and dancing. He was afraid his bachelor days would stretch far into the future, but he was wrong.

LOVE ARRIVES

When Martin graduated from Crozer Theological Seminary with his master's degree, his friends and family expected him to come home and marry a local girl. Characteristically, Martin had other ideas. As it turned out, Martin moved to Massachusetts and entered Boston College's doctoral program.

There he met a girl from Marion, Alabama. Martin fell in love with Coretta Scott from the first moment he saw her. They spent long hours studying in the library together, where Martin became more and more convinced that she was as intelligent, serious, and ambitious as she was beautiful. Coretta was in Boston studying performing arts at the New England Conservatory of Music. As the months went by and their relationship grew more serious, they both became concerned about her plans for becoming a professional singer. How could they ever combine the careers of a Baptist minister with that of a traveling concert musician? On the day Martin's parents were due to visit him in Boston and meet Coretta, he was extremely nervous.

When the doorbell rang, Coretta took hold of Martin's hand and said, "Remember, if we're to be together, it will work out." Coretta always knew just what to say to calm him. Martin realized that Coretta was the stabilizing voice he would need in his life. He loved her so much.

A they opened the door together, they heard, "Anybody home? What's wrong with these Northerners? It sure is rude to keep company waiting on the front step so long." Martin's father let out a strong, hearty laugh.

Once everyone was inside, Martin introduced his parents to Coretta. They talked about their families, their classes, and ultimately, future career goals. Martin's parents could see the tender hand touches and glances exchanged between Martin and Coretta. It was obvious to them that the relationship had already become serious. Martin and his mother soon excused themselves and went to the kitchen. Coretta shifted nervously in her seat.

Martin's father was very direct with Coretta. "Young woman, a career on the concert stage is hardly appropriate for a young woman seeing a young man from a strict Baptist upbringing and background. I believe you and M.L. are just experiencing a little infatuation that probably won't last out the school term. You would be better suited for someone within your own profession. Besides, M.L. has dated daughters of some fine, solid Atlanta families, people who have much more to offer him."

Coretta stood up. Her eyes flashed with anger, but she was determined to control her emotions, speak her mind, and still be respectful to Martin's father. "I clearly understand the sacrifice I am being asked to make," she said. "I would probably have to abandon my plans to travel and perform. My life would be totally different as a Southern pastor's wife, a mother, and a member of a tight-knit church community. Through it all, though, I know I will have plenty to offer to Martin."

Martin's father had never been

spoken to this way before, especially not by a woman. When Martin and Mrs. King entered the room again, the older man rose slowly to his feet. Everyone could feel the tension as he looked directly at Coretta and said, "Martin, I'm not exactly certain what God has planned for you, but whatever it is, you will need a wife with spunk and heart. Coretta is just that kind of girl. Besides, when you come home to Ebenezer, your mother could use some help in the music department."

On June 18, 1953, Martin and Coretta were pronounced man and wife on the lawn of her parents' home in Marion, Alabama.

MOVE TO MONTGOMERY

On a cold January morning in 1954, Martin and Coretta stood across the street looking at their first church, the Dexter Avenue Baptist Church. Martin lost no time in making changes. He had plans for getting the congregation to recruit new members from among the poorer people of the city. This last suggestion was not very popular, though.

"Dr. King, we've worked hard for years here at Dexter Avenue to try and raise the sights of our people. When we have fellowship with others of the same social status as ourselves, it is easier to run business meetings and get things done." When an elder from his church said this to him during a meeting, Martin could not believe his ears.

He looked around the room at his board of elders. He was shocked. "Gentlemen, in the midst of this heinous racial separation between

whites and Negroes in the South, I never thought I would find a greater evil. But I have. How can you possibly accept, in any form or fashion, the separation of Negroes from ourselves – and worse yet, separation along lines of class?

"We are all in the same boat. The well-dressed, college-educated Negro and the unshaven, uneducated Negro are both considered 'niggers' by white society. We cannot believe in our money. We must believe in ourselves as Men. We cannot afford to stoop to the level of our white brothers who have labeled us as less than men. How dare we do the same thing to our black brothers, just because we have bigger bank accounts?"

Under the leadership of Dr. King, Dexter Avenue Baptist Church began to change. They didn't know when or how, but they could feel that something big was about to happen.

THE BEGINNING OF A MOVEMENT

...s was a faithful member ...r of Dexter Avenue Baptist Church. Little did she know she would be the catalyst of the biggest change the South had seen since the abolition of slavery – the breakdown of the segregation system. On an ordinary day in December, 1955, Rosa left her job as seamstress in a downtown department store and got

on her bus to go home. But as the bus filled up, the driver looked back and noticed that a few white passengers had nowhere to sit. He stopped the bus and asked the blacks in the first seats behind the white section to relinquish their seats. Mrs. Parks was one of them, but she refused to move.

"No, I don't think I should have to give up my seat," she said. The bus driver asked her again, and then

called the police. A patrol car soon arrived and an officer escorted Mrs. Parks off the bus and to jail.

The black citizens of Montgomery were used to this "Jim Crow" system of laws in the South. Jim Crow laws were the ones which among other things, forced blacks to sit at the backs of buses, wait for trains in separate areas, use different and substandard restrooms, and watch movies in isolated sections of the theaters. Blacks were not allowed to vote in general elections or eat at lunch counters. In addition, black children were not allowed to attend the same schools as white children. Rosa Parks knew these laws, but on this particular day, she did not accept them. Instead she thought about young Dr. King's sermons on the need for change in their thinking, so she challenged the rules she judged to be unfair.

When the black population of Montgomery heard about the incident they felt angry enough to do something about all the injustices they were suffering. There were 48,000 blacks in the city. It was their money which kept the bus lines in business. So the city's black activists decided to organize a boycott of the city buses. At the quickly assembled meeting, Martin Luther King, Jr. was voted the head of the newly formed organization that would run the boycott – the Montgomery Improvement Association (M.I.A.).

Leaflets were quickly printed and distributed which stated, "Don't ride the bus on Monday, December 5." When Monday morning came, Martin and Coretta watched anxiously for the first bus to pass their home. Coretta noticed it first. "Look, Martin," she exclaimed, "it's empty." And so were all the others. All day long and for the weeks and months to come, the blacks of the city stayed off of the buses. The M.I.A. had organized car pools and black-run taxi companies to take people back and forth to work. Many people walked and some even used horses and buggies.

White employers threatened to fire their black employees and black taxi drivers were penalized. On Monday, January 30, 1956, about two months into the boycott, the King house was bombed. A crowd gathered and a riot threatened to break out, but Dr. King quieted the crowd. "God is with this movement. We must answer violence with nonviolence, aggression with peacefulness." With tears and nod-ding heads, the crowd went home.

By the winter of 1956 the Montgomery bus line was bankrupt. The Supreme Court finally declared segregated buses unconstitutional. It had taken more than a year, but the blacks had won their first victory over segregation in the South, nonviolent-ly. A movement had begun.

VIOLENCE AGAINST THE NONVIOLENT MOVEMENT

The first black passengers who returned to the Montgomery buses and sat wherever they wanted, met with vicious assaults from the whites. Some were called nasty names, while others were hit in the face or pushed around by white passengers. This was the repayment for their yearlong struggle. The tension could be keenly felt on buses all over the city. But the black population of Montgomery had discovered the power of nonviolence. Their reactions to these attacks were proof of their growing inner strength.

One of the members of Dr. King's church told him, "You would have been proud of Deacon Wilson. He looked the man straight in the face with his good eye as the injured one began to swell shut. They say it was silent on the bus for a good ten seconds. Then the deacon calmly took his seat – at the front of the bus, directly opposite his attacker, opened his morning paper, and began to read."

At some point, Coretta said to Martin, "This nonviolent approach is not easy. Look at all that has happened just this morning. How long will we be able to just stand and take the punishment? How long will we have to struggle against others who insist on keeping us down?"

Martin answered, "My dear, we will stand for what is right as long as it takes. They may knock us down, but we'll keep getting up. They may arrest us, but we'll keep speaking out. They may try to kill us, but the next generation will be there to carry on the struggle. You cannot kill the truth."

He had expressed these same sentiments in sermons and speeches

many times before. News of the bus boycott's success and Dr. King's amazing leadership traveled like wildfire across the country. Dr. King began to travel, spreading the message of nonviolent resistance and the Civil Rights Movement.

Late in the summer of 1958, Martin's first book, *Stride Toward Freedom* was published. He was invited to New York for an autograph session. He was surprised to hear the crowd outside booing him, even though he knew that Northern blacks were not as patient with the nonviolent message as their Southern counterparts.

Back home in Montgomery, Coretta received a distressing call from a hospital in New York. "Your husband has just arrived. He was attacked by a deranged woman at the autograph session."

"Is he all right? Please, is he alive?" Coretta's voice trembled.

"Oh yes, ma'am. But the stab wound was made by a letter opener that is still in his chest, so we must operate." The delicate operation lasted several hours. The tip of the letter opener had been so close to his heart that if Martin had coughed, it could have meant his death.

While Martin was recovering, he and Coretta noticed a change in the way the Northerners were now willing to accept him. The quiet manner in which he had handled this crisis had proven his method to them. He was now being compared to Gandhi. He and Coretta decided to travel to India so they could find out more about the nonviolent movement going on there.

India's Caste System and Segregation in America's South

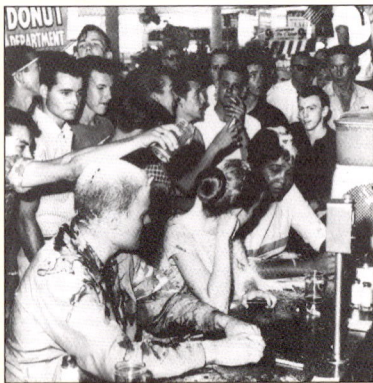

In India during the first half of this century there was a strict system of social separation known as the caste system. People were divided into groups so that the very rich were considered better than those with less money. They were allowed many more privileges. For example, thousands of India's lowest caste, known as the Untouchables, starved to death every year, whereas the higher castes had an overabundance of food. The caste system was supported and endorsed by the government of India.

Mahatma Gandhi was a man who dreamed of a truly united India, Muslims living in peace with Hindus and Christians, free from the unfair caste system. He felt that the people who were being hurt the most should do something about the way they were being treated. He had preached that nonviolent resistance against the injustices of the caste system could bring about a change. By resisting the government's unjust laws without violence, many changes were made in India.

Dr. King saw a parallel between the caste system in India and the Jim Crow system of the South. He believed that if nonviolent resistance could work to break down the caste system in India, it could work to break down segregation in the South.

Left: *Sit-in demonstrators harrassed by angry white youths in North Carolina, 1960.* Above: *MLK and wife Coretta lead march in Selma, Alabama, March 1965.*

INJUSTICE REMAINS

When Dr. King returned from India, he felt more strongly than ever that nonviolent resistance was the best possible means of bringing about social change. In 1960, he and his family returned to Atlanta where he assisted his father in the pulpit of Ebenezer Baptist Church. With renewed vigor, he spoke at church services and rallies all over the country. As president of the Southern Christian Leadership Council (SCLC), he continued to direct the staging of bus boycotts in cities throughout the South. Yes, the message of the need for social equality had caught on, but the tone of the movement began to change. Young people, both blacks and whites, were beginning to force confrontation by directly disobeying unjust laws through actions such as sit-ins and the "Freedom Rides." This drew violence from those who disagreed with racial equality.

The day finally came when Martin was arrested and thrown into jail.

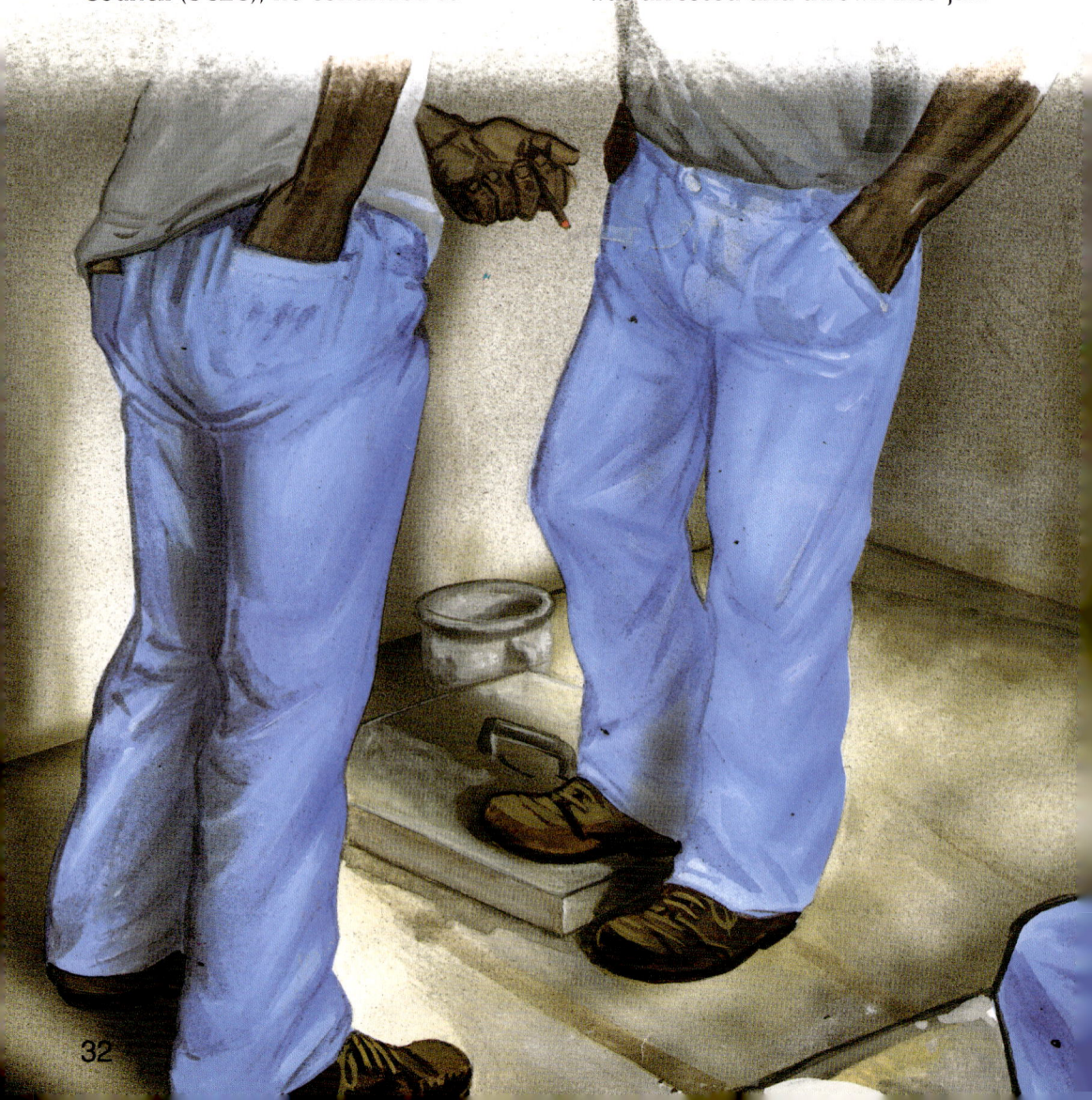

Martin's father found the phone number of the judge and called him right away. "Judge Mitchell, this is Reverend Martin King, Sr. I understand that you have seen my son this evening."

"Why Dr. King, it seems your son didn't transfer his driver's license from Alabama to Georgia. Shame, shame."

"Surely, you cannot expect to hold and convict him on something as insignificant as a traffic charge."

"I've sentenced your precious son to four months at hard labor. Maybe some time in chains will teach him his place."

News of Dr. King's arrest traveled fast. His father contacted a prominent Atlanta attorney who had political connections and soon the White House also knew what was going on. President Eisenhower and Vice-President Nixon thought it over, but decided they should not get involved. It was a state problem.

Coretta was extremely upset about the turn of events. She knew how her husband hated isolation. Besides, he

The Freedom Rides

The year was 1961. The purpose of the Freedom Rides was the desegregation of interstate buses. Martin Luther King, Jr. was the chairman of the SNCC,

the group organizing these rides. White and black passengers would ride on Greyhound and Trailways buses, then get off them at stations and make a point of mixing and using the same dining room and restroom facilities.

The first Freedom Riders left Washington, D.C. and planned to travel through Virginia, North Carolina, South Carolina, Georgia, Alabama, and Mississippi. Everything went fine at first, but the deeper into the South the buses went, the more violent the white reaction grew. In Rock Hill, South Carolina, and

Anniston and Birmingham, Alabama, mobs savagely beat the passengers trying to get off the buses.

Despite the opposition, change did come about because of the Freedom Rides. In November 1961, the Interstate Commerce Commission ruled against segregation on all interstate vehicles and in public facilities.

would worry about how all this was affecting her. She was pregnant with their third child. Then, just when everything seemed so hopeless, she received an unexpected call from John F. Kennedy, the senator from Massachusetts. "Mrs. King," she could hear his Boston accent clearly, "I want to express my extreme concern over the imprisonment of your husband. I am alarmed over the clear violation of law that has taken place in this case. My brother Robert, has considerable influence with Judge Mitchell. He is contacting the judge and I am sure a change is forthcoming. Our prayers are with you."

Judge Mitchell's telephone rang again. "This is Robert Kennedy." The judge's eyes grew big. "Why hasn't bail been granted in the King case? No serious crime is involved. Washington is very interested in how you are handling things there." In no time at all papers were signed ordering Dr. King's release for the very next day.

The political friends Dr. King had in John and Robert Kennedy solidified his position as national leader of the Civil Rights Movement. Martin realized that fewer than five per cent of the American black population (22 million) were actively participating in the movement. So, after John F. Kennedy was elected president of the United States, Dr. King decided it was time to take the Civil Rights Movement to all of America in a big way.

Letter From a Birmingham Jail

Martin Luther King, Jr. was arrested many times for disobeying unjust laws. One time he was arrested in Birmingham, Alabama for leading a march that had been forbidden by a court injunction. Birmingham was known as the meanest city in the South, but segregation was just as wrong there as in any other Southern city. Dr. King was thrown into solitary confinement in a cell with no mattress, pillow or blanket and subjected to extremely abusive language by his jailers. He was held from Good Friday, April 12, 1963 until Easter Sunday, April 14, without being allowed to make any calls or have any visitors.

His wife Coretta, got very worried so she called President Kennedy for help. Robert Kennedy returned her call because the President was out, but he assured her that her husband was all right. The next day, the President himself called her to say that he had talked personally with officials in Birmingham. He assured her that she would soon receive a call from her husband.

Dr. King wondered why the guards changed and suddenly became so polite. When they allowed him to call his wife, he found out that she had requested and received help directly from President Kennedy. He asked her to let everyone know that the president was watching Birmingham. Then he set about to put his time to good use.

While in jail, he wrote a 6,400-word essay that has become known as the famous "Letter from Birmingham Jail." The following is an excerpt from that letter:

"One may well ask, 'How can you advocate breaking some laws and obeying others?' The answer lies in the fact that there are two types of laws: just and unjust. I would be the first to advocate obeying just laws. One has not only a legal, but a moral responsibility to obey just laws. Conversely, one has a moral responsibility to disobey unjust laws. . . . Oppressed people cannot remain oppressed forever. The urge for freedom will eventually come. This is what happened to the American Negro. Something within has reminded him of his birthright of freedom; something without has reminded him that he can gain it."

"I HAVE A DREAM"

By 1963, Martin and Coretta had four children, Yolanda Denise, Martin III, Dexter Scott, and Bernice. The couple taught their children to love Jesus just as their parents had taught them. In light of the life they led as the family of Martin Luther King, Jr., they had more than their share of opportunities to put the truth of the Bible to the test.

One night Martin could see there was something bothering his oldest son, Martin III. When he asked the boy what was the matter, tears began to flow down little Martin's cheeks. He blurted his answer in a way that

shocked everyone around the table. "I don't understand! You tell Negroes not to fight back. But I've seen the mobs and the police on T.V. They beat the Freedom Riders and turn fire hoses full force on peaceful marchers. How can I bless those people? They hate us. And it looks like they'll never change."

Dr. King stayed calm. He understood his son's frustration. He had felt the same when he was a boy. "Times are changing, son. It takes time, but little by little, our persistence upon that which is right and true, is breaking down the walls of separation. Things are better for me than they were for my father. I'm involved in this struggle because I want America to be an even better place for you. Hating our enemies makes us just like them. God knew what He was talking about. Blessing our enemies beats them with a weapon stronger than any other – love. Do you understand now, son?"

Martin III ran around the table to hug his father. That night, Dr. King was preparing his speech to be delivered at the long-planned "March on Washington." He may have had conversations with his children like the one above in mind when he wrote the following section of his famous "I Have a Dream" speech:

"I have a dream my four little children will one day live in a nation where they will not be judged by the color of their skin, but by the content of their character. I have a dream today! . . . And when we allow freedom to ring, when we let it ring from every village and hamlet, from every state and city, we will be able to speed up that day when all of God's children – black men and white men, Jews and Gentiles, Protestants and Catholics – will be able to join hands and to sing in the words of the old Negro spiritual, 'Free at last, free at last; thank God Almighty, we're free at last.'"

The March on Washington

occupations – marched from the Washington Monument to the Lincoln Memorial in order to "arouse the conscience of the nation over the economic plight of the Negro."

It was a hot summer afternoon and the heat was taking its toll on the gigantic crowd. At around 3 p.m., everyone stood listening to the beautiful contralto voice of gospel singer Mahalia Jackson. After she sang "I've Been 'Buked and I've Been Scorned," the crowd turned its attention to

74-year-old A. Philip Randolph. He introduced Dr. Martin Luther King, Jr. as "the moral leader of the nation."

The speech Dr. King delivered on that day was not very long, but what it lacked in length it made up for in power.

Although Dr. King's dream would not be fully realized for many years, history will never be able to forget the movement or the man who stated so eloquently, "I have a dream today!"

The "I Have a Dream Speech."

Back in 1941 A. Philip Randolph had had a vision of a massive, nonviolent, dignified parade marching through the nation's capital in favor of civil rights. That parade never materialized, but on August 28, 1963, nearly 250,000 people – all of different ethnic backgrounds, ages, and

Significant Court and Congressional Acts

Important Dates

1956
U.S. District and Supreme Court rule that segregation on city bus lines is unconstitutional.

1960 Civil Rights Act calls for:
1. Penalties for obstructing school desegregation orders.
2. Preservation of voting records.
3. Strengthening civil rights act of 1957.

1964 Civil Rights Act calls for:
1. Equal access to public accommodations.
2. Desegregation of public facilities and schools.
3. Equal employment.
4. Nondiscrimination in federally assisted programs.

1965
Voting Rights Act authorizes federal examiners to register black voters at the state level.

1966
Civil Rights Bill bans racial discrimination in the sale and/or rental of housing.

1968
Civil Rights Act places a federal ban on housing discrimination

President Lyndon B. Johnson signs Civil Rights Act, July 2, 1964. Luther King, Jr. is standing behind the president.

THE NOBEL PEACE PRIZE

The March on Washington was an overwhelming success. It alerted the entire nation to the plight of blacks in the South, and to the unjust laws and attitudes against blacks all over the country. The wheels of the legislative process were turning to get a sweeping Civil Rights Bill passed and added to the Constitution of the United States.

Then the hopes of the movement were temporarily dashed on November 22, 1963 – just three short months after the March on Washington – when President John F. Kennedy was killed by an assassin's bullet. The movement had lost a staunch ally, but Dr. King continued

leading the struggle and his efforts did not go unnoticed.

The telephone rang at the residence of Reverend King, Sr. "Hi, Dad. It's Martin." Father and son always enjoyed talking to each other. "I've been thinking. You need a vacation."

"Do I?" answered Martin's father. "And where do you propose that I go?"

"I think you and Mom would enjoy seeing Oslo, Norway."

"We don't know anybody in Oslo, Norway. Why would we want to go there? M.L., what are you up to?"

"Well, Dad, I just thought you might like to attend the ceremony where they hand out the Nobel Peace Prize. They tell me that's where I have to go to pick it up."

There was a pause on the other end of the line.

"Dad, are you still there?" Dr. King asked.

"Son, I'm so glad I lived to see this moment. I'm so proud of you."

"I knew you would be, Dad. This award is just as much yours as it is mine. You taught me how to have the dream. Will you go? Tell Christine and A.D. The children will stay home, but I want the rest of my family with me."

So on December 10, 1964, Dr. Martin Luther King, Jr. received the Nobel Peace Prize for his efforts towards racial peace and unity.

Notable American Nobel Prize Laureates

1906 *Theodore Roosevelt* (honored for bringing Russo-Japanese war to an end).
1919 *Woodrow Wilson* (establishment of League of Nations).
1925 *Charles Dawes* (helped readmit Germany into European fraternity; healing after the war).
1931 *Nicholas Murray Butler* (fighting to make the world safe for democracy).
1946 *John R. Mott* (organized Christian Student Union and Intercollegiate Young Men's Christian Association (YMCA)).
1950 *Ralph J. Bunche* (negotiation between Israel and four Arab neighbors).
1962 *Linus Carl Pauling* (work against atomic warfare).
1964 *Martin Luther King, Jr.* (fight for Civil Rights for American blacks).

THE LAST FOUR, HARD YEARS

When they returned from Oslo, Coretta said to Martin, "You know Martin, the Nobel Peace Prize is the most significant recognition you have received for your work. Things might get easier for us now. After all, the whole world knows about the movement now."

But it was not to be. The next four years were as full of turmoil as they were triumphs. Events seemed to unfold so rapidly that it was hard to keep up with them.

February 21, 1965: Just two months after Dr. King received the Nobel Peace Prize, a prominent black leader, Malcolm X, was shot and killed.

March 7, 1965: Two weeks after Malcolm X's assassination, a situation that had been brewing in Selma, Alabama came to a head. The Student Nonviolent Coordinating Committee (SNCC) had been making progress in registering black voters, but police had been called in with guard dogs to force marchers and

their children away from the steps of the capitol building

August 6, 1965: The Voting Rights Bill was signed into law.

August 11, 1965: The Watts section of Los Angeles, California, erupted in riots. Martin said to Coretta that night, "I was afraid it would come to this. Once a people have learned to see injustice for what it really is, they can tolerate it only so long. Racial hatred is breaking this country apart. Will the country have to be literally burned to the ground before it can be rebuilt into somewhere worthwhile to live?"

Summer 1966: Riots were breaking out in various cities across America. The movement was being met with stringent opposition, especially in all-white neighborhoods. Dr. King still felt the nonviolent approach could win out over the violence exploding all around him. He took on the Chicago slum problem by moving into a slum apartment to publicize the plight of blacks in urban centers around the country.

By 1967, Dr. King was speaking out against the war in Vietnam. His non-violent stand was not something he checked at the border, and this cost him the support of the administration under President Lyndon Johnson.

April 1968: The sanitation workers in Memphis, Tennessee, went on strike because of low pay and other unfair conditions. Most of the sanitation workers in the city were black, and since the city was ignoring their demands, they called on Dr. King. Despite his heavy schedule, he felt the need to answer their call. It was the last aid he would ever give.

LOOKING BACK— LOOKING AHEAD

In his book *Daddy King*, Reverend King, Sr. remembers April 4, 1968: "We went upstairs to my study and I turned on the radio. The newscaster had a final, somber bulletin: Martin Luther King, Jr. had been shot to death while standing on a balcony at the Lorraine Motel in Memphis. I turned to Bunch (Mrs. King, Sr.). Neither of us could say anything. Suddenly, in a few seconds of radio time, it was over. My first son, whose

birth had brought me such joy that I jumped up in the hall outside the room where he was born and touched the ceiling – the child, the scholar, the preacher, the boy singing and smiling, the son – all of it was gone."

Dr. Benjamin Mays had challenged and taught the young Martin Luther King, Jr. while he was a student at Morehouse. He remembers Martin's intensity. He stayed in contact with Martin throughout his life and recalls:

"Segregation went unchallenged until 1955. King went to Montgomery to relax and finish his Ph.D. dissertation. One week after he mailed it in, Rosa Parks sat down in the front of the bus. King was destined to lead a great movement. He once said, 'You are God's children and every man from a bass black to a treble white is significant on God's keyboard.' Martin devoted his life to bringing about the recognition of the significance of the American Negro. . . . It's the teachings of Jesus; right there in the New Testament. . . . We've preached it and talked about it for a long time. But it was talk and no action. He made it walk on the ground."

Significant Marches, Boycotts, Campaigns and Movements

The Montgomery Bus Boycott. Began December 5, 1955 and lasted over a year.

Prayer Pilgrimage in Washington 1957.

Interracial Youth March 1958. Dramatized support for school integration.

Student sit-ins 1960. Student Nonviolent Coordinating Committee (SNCC) staged protests across the South.

Freedom Rides. Began May 4, 1961 for the purpose of desegregating interstate buses and terminals.

Birmingham Movement 1963. Dr. King jailed; wrote "Letter from Birmingham Jail."

The Children's Crusade 1963.

March on Washington 1963. Dr. King delivered famous "I Have a Dream" speech.

St. Augustine campaign 1964. Focused on the issue of states' rights.

Mississippi Freedom Summer 1964. Students focused on lack of opportunities and justice in Deep South states.

Selma Campaign 1965. Voter registration drive.

Bloody Sunday 1965. Turning point when many from all races joined Freedom Movement.

March from Selma to Montgomery 1965.

Chicago Movement 1966. Called attention to conditions in city ghettos.

Poor People's March 1967. Highlighted need for jobs and freedom among black and white poor people.

Memphis 1968. Striking sanitation workers needed help.

And walk they did. On Monday, April 8, 1968, the nonviolent march that Dr. King had planned was held as scheduled with Coretta Scott King, the slain leader's wife, walking in her husband's place. The next day, hundreds of thousands of mourners followed Dr. King's body as it was carried through the streets of Atlanta on a mule-drawn farm wagon. Mrs. King

chose to honor him in this way because he had represented the simple, common people during his life.

The bullet fired from the rifle of James Earl Ray may have ended the life of Dr. Martin Luther King, Jr., but it could not snuff out his dream. Thousands of people continued the struggle to ensure that blacks continued to receive their rights. Hundreds of schools, buildings, streets, and parks across America were renamed in his honor. And although it took eighteen years, on January 15, 1986, Dr. King's birthday was declared a national holiday – America's first official national holiday in honor of a black American. Dr. Martin Luther King, Jr., a great man, a great American, a great Christian.

Main Events in Luther King's Life

1929 MLK born January 15.

1944 MLK enters Morehouse College, age 15.

1948 MLK ordained a Baptist minister.

1951 MLK graduates from Crozer.

1953 MLK marries Coretta Scott, June 18.

1954 MLK installed as pastor of Dexter Avenue Baptist Church.

1955 MLK gets his Ph.D. in systematic theology from Boston University.

1955 Yolanda King born Nov. 17.

1955 Rosa Parks arrested for violating Montgomery's bus segregation ordinance, Dec. 1.

1955 Montgomery Bus Boycott begins, Dec. 5.

1956 Federal and Supreme courts rule bus segregation is unconstitutional.

1957 SCLC formed, Feb. 14.

1957 MLK III born, Oct. 23.

1958 MLK's 'Stride Toward Freedom' published, Sept. 17.

1958 MLK stabbed in Harlem, Dec. 19.

1959 MLK's trip to India.

1960 MLK becomes co-pastor at Ebenezer Baptist Church, Jan.

1961 Dexter King born, Jan. 30.

1961 Freedom Rides bagin, Mar.

1963 Bernice King born, Mar.28.

1963 MLK writes "Letter from a Birmingham Jail."

1963 March on Washington; "I Have a Dream" speech, Aug. 28.

1964 MLK awarded Nobel Peace Prize in Oslo, Dec. 10.

1965 MLK leads Selma-to-Montgomery march, urges marchers to turn back, Mar. 9.

1965 Voting Rights Bill signed into law, Aug. 6.

1966 MLK moves into a slum apartment in Chicago.

1967 MLK first denounces Vietnam War.

1968 MLK leads a demonstration in Memphis that turns violent, Mar. 28.

1968 MLK's `Mountaintop' speech in Memphis, Apr. 3.

1968 MLK assassinated in Memphis, Apr. 4.

1968 MLK's funeral, Apr. 9.

1986 Dr. King's birthday officially celebrated as a national holiday (first holiday in US to honor a Black American).

THE AMERICAN SOUTH

BOOK RESOURCES

Martin Luther King, Jr. and the March Toward Freedom, by Rita Hakim (The Millbrook Press, 1991).
The Life and Death of Martin Luther King, Jr., by James Haskins (Lothrop, Lee & Shepard Co., 1977).
My Life With Martin Luther King, Jr., by Coretta Scott King (Henry Holt and Company, 1993).
Daddy King, An Autobiography, by Martin Luther King, Sr., with Clayton Riley (William Morrow and Company, 1980).
Voice of Deliverance, by Keith D. Miller (Macmillan, 1992).
Martin Luther King, Jr. and the Freedom Movement, by Lillie Patterson (Facts On File, 1989).
Martin Luther King, Jr., His Religion, His Philosophy (Exposition Press of Florida, 1986).